ice cream

ice cream

Liz Franklin

photography by William Lingwood

RYLAND
PETERS
& SMALL

LONDON NEW YORK

Commissioning Editor
Elsa Petersen-Schepelern

Production Jacquie Horner

Art Director Gabriella Le Grazie

Publishing Director Alison Starling

Food Stylist Liz Franklin

Prop Stylist Chloe Brown

First published in
Great Britain in 2005
by Ryland Peters & Small
20–21 Jockey's Fields
London WC1R 4BW
www.rylandpeters.com

10 9 8 7 6 5 4 3 2

Text © Liz Franklin 2005
Design and photographs
© Ryland Peters & Small 2005

ISBN 1 84172 821 7

A catalogue record for this
book is available from the
British Library.

For Michelle

NOTES

- All spoon measurements are level unless otherwise stated.
- Eggs are large unless otherwise specified. Uncooked or partly cooked eggs should not be served to the very old, frail, young children, pregnant women or those with compromised immune systems.

Author's acknowledgements

With huge thanks to the wonderful team at RP&S, in particular the lovely Elsa, for asking me to write this book, thereby allowing me to indulge myself in the guilt-free consumption of ice cream during its writing. To Paul, for the chuckles, the encouragement and the beautiful design that made this a book of which I am very proud. Thanks too to William Lingwood, for his patience and beautiful photography – and to Estelle for the giggles and great lunches at the shoots! My thanks and my love also go out to my dear and much-missed friend Michelle, who gave me my first ever 'proper' ice cream machine all those years ago, and to my sons Chris, Oli and Tim who keep me on my ice cream toes with their continuing enthusiasm and appetite for homemade ice cream! Big hugs to my mum and dad for magical ice cream memories and special thanks to my many wonderful friends who tasted and tested along the way, in particular Jan, Patricia and Rosie – and to PJ too – for helping with the words, when I sometimes couldn't find them.

contents

have fun freezing ...

I've always adored ice cream. As a small child, the tinkling chimes of the ice cream van were the signal to run out to buy a cornet topped with a whirl of light-as-air ice cream and a chocolate flake.

Years passed, but my enthusiasm for ice cream continued. At college in the seaside town of Scarborough, hardly a day went by without a visit to the harbour-front ice cream parlour for a regular treat – two doorstep-sized chocolate wafers sandwiching a flurry of white-as-snow ice cream.

My happy habit continued, until I bought an ice cream on a marina in Portugal. The cone was made from crisp waffled biscuit and was almost the size of the Olympic torch. It would easily have outfaced me, had it not been filled with the most exquisite ice cream I had ever tasted. Not whipped and white this time, but dense, delicious and the colour of rich cream. It was flecked with the tiny black seeds from plump Madagascan vanilla pods and each mouthful was pure bliss. This was real ice cream – and so began my ongoing love affair with homemade ice cream.

I started by making the easiest of all Italian ice creams, semifreddo, a meringue-like cloud of whipped egg whites folded into a delicious creamy base, which prevents the mixture from freezing completely solid. The result is a soft-scoop ice that doesn't need a machine. I was delighted with the results and thrilled with the compliments. Keen to try out other ice creams and sorbets, I invested in the most basic of electric ice cream machines – the kind where the bowl is stored in the freezer until just before churning.

Over the years, I have used several excellent machines and all of them have more than earned their keep. I am delighted that my current machine is restaurant-grade!

An ice cream can capture summer in a cone or add something special to a hot winter pudding. A sorbet or slush can solve the problem of something light and luscious to end a substantial meal. Simple or sophisticated, ices make a tempting treat for all ages.

Commercially made, chemically enhanced ice creams can never compare with those made at home with fresh, natural ingredients. Premium-grade commercial ice creams do contain better ingredients, but they are expensive and flavours are limited.

So here I am, sharing my favourite frozen treasures, in the hope that you will love and use them every bit as much as I do!

Have fun freezing!

equipment

Electric ice cream machines

An electric ice cream machine is a blessing for people who make their own ice cream regularly. Your choice of machine will be influenced by the number of times it will be used – and cost. The most basic electric machine is made up of a main body housing a motor and paddle unit. A separate gel-filled inner bowl is placed in a freezer overnight, then removed and attached to the motor unit when the mixture is ready to be frozen. The disadvantage with this type of machine is that the inner bowl has to be refrozen after each batch of ice cream.

Spend five or six times this amount, and you can buy a machine with a built-in self-freezing unit. This type of machine will churn about a litre at a time and be capable of making further batches immediately.

Making ice cream by hand

You can also make good ice cream without a machine. It takes longer and requires more elbow grease, but you will still be rewarded for your efforts. The mixture should be frozen in a shallow container. When almost solid, beat it well with a wire whisk or electric beater until smooth, then return to the freezer. Repeat the process twice more to break down the ice crystals, and the result will be a smooth, silky ice cream.

After freezing, all ice creams should be stored in well-sealed, freezer-proof containers to prevent freezer burn. Delicate ice creams will easily take up flavours from other foods stored nearby, so tight-fitting lids are important.

Homemade ice cream is best eaten as soon as possible after being made, and certainly within a week if possible – besides, you'll love it so much, it won't linger that long.

As a general rule, ice cream should be transferred to the refrigerator for 20–30 minutes before serving, to let it soften evenly throughout and be perfect to eat!

Scoops

Dip ice cream scoops into iced water just before using – this will make the surface of the ice cream smoother. There are three kinds – one is a basic curved spoon, another a flat paddle used in the gelaterias in Italy, while a third has a lever mechanism operated through the handle. All are good, though I find that an ordinary tablespoon dipped in water works just as well if you don't have a special scoop.

ingredients

As in all cooking, the quality of ingredients will be reflected in the finished results, and none more so than in ice cream making.

Eggs

I use large, free-range, organic eggs. Uncooked or partly cooked eggs should not be served to the very old, frail, young children, pregnant women or those with compromised immune systems.

Cream

I always use fresh double cream, Italian mascarpone cheese, whole milk and full-fat yoghurts. Using skimmed dairy products compromises flavour and texture – much better to enjoy something special and eat a little less.

Sugar

I use caster sugar instead of granulated, because it has a much finer texture and gives a smoother result. To achieve a deeper flavour in some recipes, I have used light or dark muscovado sugar. Light adds a delicate toffee flavour, dark will add an intense caramel flavour.

mascarpone ice cream

This lovely, light, milky ice cream – wonderful on its own – is also an excellent base for delicate flavours that would be masked by a rich egg custard.

Put the mascarpone, milk and sugar in a bowl and whisk until thick and smooth. Transfer to an ice cream machine and churn until frozen.

Transfer to a freezer-proof container and freeze until ready to serve. Alternatively, to freeze without a machine, see page 8.

250 g mascarpone cheese
250 ml whole milk
150 g caster sugar

an ice cream machine (optional)

SERVES 4–6

ice cream

rich vanilla ice cream

Studded with tiny, perfumed seeds, the vanilla pod belongs to the orchid family. Madagascan vanilla is highly regarded and is easily found in good food shops, but the finest in the world is believed to be Bourbon. Real vanilla is expensive, but the process that takes it from plant to table is so complex, there is little wonder. Don't be tempted to save money by using cheap, inferior imitation vanilla, the results simply won't be the same. However, do rinse and dry the pods, then bury them deep in a jar of sugar to flavour it in readiness for your next batch of ice cream.

2 vanilla pods

300 ml whole milk

300 ml double cream

6 large egg yolks

150 g caster sugar

an ice cream machine (optional)

SERVES 4–6

Slit the vanilla pods in half lengthways and scrape out the seeds with the tip of a sharp knife. Put the pods in a saucepan and the seeds in a bowl.

Pour the milk and cream into the saucepan and bring just to boiling point. Remove from the heat and set aside to infuse for at least 30 minutes.

Put the eggs and sugar in a bowl and beat until pale and creamy. Return the cream mixture to the heat and bring back to the boil. Pour the hot liquid over the eggs, stir until smooth, then pour back into the pan. Reduce the heat and cook over low heat, stirring constantly with a wooden spoon, until the custard has thickened enough to leave a finger trail on the back of the spoon. Take care that the mixture doesn't overheat and scramble.

Let the custard cool completely, then churn in an ice cream machine and transfer to a freezer-proof container and freeze until ready to serve. Alternatively, to freeze without a machine, see page 8.

Note If you have time, the custard will benefit by being left for several hours before churning, to let the flavours develop fully.

caramel ice cream

Caramel always seems to be high on everyone's list of most-loved ice cream flavours, and this is so easy to make, it's sure to become a favourite. Just take care when adding the cold cream to the hot caramel – the mixture can tend to splutter and caramel can cause nasty burns if it comes into contact with skin.

200 g caster sugar

600 ml double cream

150 ml whole milk

6 egg yolks, beaten

a sugar thermometer (optional)

a pastry brush

an ice cream machine (optional)

SERVES 4–6

Put the sugar in a heavy saucepan over medium heat and cook until the sugar dissolves completely. Increase the heat and bubble the mixture until it develops a dark amber colour – 154°C (310°F) on a sugar thermometer. Use a pastry brush dampened with a little water to wash down the sides of the pan and prevent burning.

When the sugar has reached the desired colour, carefully pour in the cream. The mixture may spit and seize at this stage. Return the mixture to the stove and stir over low heat until the caramel has dissolved thoroughly in the cream. Let cool.

Heat the milk in a separate saucepan until boiling. Remove from the heat and pour it slowly into the beaten egg, stirring until smooth. Pour the mixture back into the pan and cook over low heat until it thickens to the texture of pouring cream. Let cool completely, then stir into the caramel mixture. Churn in an ice cream machine, transfer to a freezer-proof container and freeze until ready to serve.

Alternatively, to freeze without a machine, see page 8.

cherry fudge ice cream

It can be a difficult task for a fudge addict like me to make this ice cream without seriously diminishing the required weight of fudge before the time comes to add it to the base mix. What makes this ice cream such a winner is the generous speckling of chewy fudge and cherries dotted throughout, so I suggest that you do as I have learned to do – play safe and always buy extra fudge to nibble on.

250 g mascarpone cheese

250 ml whole milk

150 g caster sugar

200 g soft fudge, cut into chunks

100 g glacé cherries, halved

an ice cream machine (optional)

SERVES 4–6

Put the mascarpone, milk and sugar in a bowl and whisk until smooth. Transfer the mixture to an ice cream machine and churn until almost frozen.

Add the fudge pieces and the chopped cherries and continue churning until the mixture is completely frozen. Transfer to a freezer-proof container and freeze until ready to serve.

If you are making the ice cream without a machine, follow the instructions on page 8 and fold in the fudge pieces and chopped cherries before returning the ice cream to the freezer for the final time.

chocolate chip cookie ice cream

Choose good-quality cookies, made with butter if possible – and of course, plenty of real chocolate chips. Cheaper cookies will spoil the ice cream by giving it a greasy aftertaste when frozen.

Put the mascarpone, milk and sugar in a bowl and whisk until smooth. Transfer the mixture to an ice cream machine and churn until almost frozen.

Fold in the crumbled cookies and continue churning until the mixture is completely frozen. Transfer to a freezer-proof container and freeze until ready to serve.

If you are making the ice cream without a machine, follow the instructions on page 8 and fold in the crumbled cookies before returning the ice cream to the freezer for the final time.

250 g mascarpone cheese

250 ml whole milk

100 g light muscovado sugar

150 g chocolate chip cookies, crumbled

an ice cream machine (optional)

SERVES 4–6

fresh peach ice cream

A perfect sun-ripened peach has to be one of summer's great treats. Firm, yet oozing sweet juices and full of flavour, they make delectable eating – and this is the best time for putting them into ice cream too. In reality, they can vary hugely in flavour, so don't be afraid to adjust the amount of sugar in the recipe to compensate if needed. The mixture should taste slightly over-sweetened before churning, because freezing will dampen down the effect of the sugar.

Put the peaches in a food processor, add the mascarpone, milk, sugar and vodka, if using, and blend to a smooth, thick purée. Churn in an ice cream machine, then transfer to a freezer-proof container and freeze until ready to serve.

Alternatively, to freeze without a machine, see page 8.

4 ripe juicy peaches, halved and stoned

250 g mascarpone cheese

200 ml whole milk

200 g caster sugar

3 tablespoons vodka (optional)

a food processor

an ice cream machine (optional)

SERVES 4–6

new york cheesecake ice cream

All the flavours of a luscious, lemony New York cheesecake, right down to the crunch of the cookie base. Don't be tempted to use low-fat cream cheese – the flavour and texture won't be the same. Just eat, enjoy, and power-walk to work tomorrow!

Pour the milk and cream into a saucepan and heat to boiling point.

Put the eggs and sugar in a bowl and beat until pale and creamy. Pour the hot liquid over the eggs, stir until smooth, then pour back into the saucepan. Turn down the heat and cook over low heat, stirring constantly with a wooden spoon, until the custard has thickened enough to leave a finger trail on the back of the spoon. Take care that the mixture doesn't overheat and scramble.

Remove from the heat and let cool completely. Beat in the cream cheese and the lemon juice and zest until smooth. Churn in an ice cream machine until the mixture is almost frozen. Add the crumbled cookies and continue to churn until it is completely frozen. Transfer to a freezer-proof container and freeze until ready to serve.

If you are making the ice cream without a machine, follow the instructions on page 8 and fold in the crumbled cookies before returning the ice cream to the freezer for the final time.

100 ml whole milk

100 ml double cream

4 egg yolks

150 g caster sugar

300 g cream cheese

grated zest and freshly squeezed juice of 2 unwaxed lemons

100 g oat cookies, crumbled into small pieces

an ice cream machine (optional)

SERVES 4–6

buttered pecan and maple syrup ice cream

Toasting the pecans in butter gives them delicious flavour, but don't allow yourself to be distracted during the process – sizzling nuts wait for no man (or woman!)

2 tablespoons unsalted butter

150 g pecan nuts, coarsely chopped

300 ml whole milk

300 ml double cream

6 egg yolks

100 g soft light brown sugar

150 ml maple syrup

an ice cream machine (optional)

SERVES 4–6

Melt the butter in a heavy saucepan, add the pecans and fry gently over low heat until golden and fragrant. Remove to a plate and let cool.

Pour the milk and cream into a separate saucepan and bring to the boil. Put the egg yolks and sugar in a bowl and beat until smooth. Pour the hot liquid over the eggs, stir until smooth, then return to the saucepan. Turn down the heat and cook over low heat, stirring constantly, until the custard has thickened, taking care not to let the mixture overheat and scramble. Add the maple syrup and let cool completely.

Churn in an ice cream machine until almost frozen. Add the chopped pecans and continue to churn until the mixture is completely frozen. Transfer to a freezer-proof container and freeze until ready to serve.

If you are making the ice cream without a machine, follow the instructions on page 8 and fold in the pecans just before returning the ice cream to the freezer for the final time.

dark chocolate mint crackle ice cream

I'm sometimes asked how I judge the amount of each ingredient to start with when I develop recipes from scratch. Here, it happened by chance. Trying to re-create the flavour of my favourite crackly after-dinner mints in an ice cream, I started with two 100 g bars of very tempting dark chocolate. Then I ate two squares. By a stroke of luck, I seemed to be left with the perfect quantity to produce this deliciously different ice cream.

180 g dark chocolate, with at least 70 per cent cocoa solids

100 g caster sugar

3 tablespoons crème de cacao (optional but delicious)

3–4 tablespoons Demerara sugar

a small bunch fresh mint, finely chopped

an ice cream machine (optional)

SERVES 4–6

Melt the chocolate, caster sugar and 200 ml water in a heatproof bowl set over a saucepan of simmering water, or microwave on HIGH for 1 minute. Add the crème de cacao, if using, then let cool completely. Churn in an ice cream machine until almost frozen. Add the Demerara sugar and chopped mint and continue to churn until the mixture is completely frozen. Transfer to a freezer-proof container and freeze until ready to serve.

If you are making the ice cream without a machine, follow the instructions on page 8 and fold in the Demerara and mint just before returning the ice cream to the freezer for the final time.

peanut brittle ice cream

Rather than raw peanuts in their skins, use ready roasted, lightly salted peanuts. The small amount of salt on the nuts seems to enhance the flavour. Keep a couple of tablespoons of the brittle to sprinkle over the ice cream when serving.

300 ml whole milk

300 ml double cream

6 egg yolks

150 g caster sugar

peanut brittle

150 g caster sugar

150 g peanuts (see recipe introduction)

a pastry brush

a sugar thermometer (optional)

a baking sheet, lightly buttered

an ice cream machine (optional)

SERVES 4–6

To make the peanut brittle, put the sugar and 100 ml water in a heavy saucepan over low heat and cook until the sugar has completely dissolved. Use a pastry brush dampened with a little water to wash down the sides of the pan and prevent burning.

Increase the heat and bubble the mixture until it develops a dark amber colour – 154°C (310°F) on a sugar thermometer. Stir in the peanuts, then immediately pour the mixture onto the prepared baking sheet. Let cool completely, then break into small pieces.

To make the ice cream, pour the milk and cream into a saucepan and heat to boiling point.

Put the eggs and sugar in a bowl and beat until smooth. Pour the hot liquid over the eggs, stir until smooth, then return the mixture to the saucepan. Turn down the heat and cook over low heat, stirring constantly with a wooden spoon, until the custard has thickened enough to leave a finger trail on the back of the spoon. Take care that the mixture doesn't overheat and scramble.

Let the custard cool completely. Churn in an ice cream machine until almost frozen. Add the broken peanut brittle and continue to churn until the mixture is completely frozen. Transfer to a freezer-proof container and freeze until ready to serve.

If you are making the ice cream without a machine, follow the instructions on page 8 and fold in the crushed peanut brittle just before returning the ice cream to the freezer for the final time.

sherry and raisin ice cream

On a trip to Spain's sherry-making region several years ago, I fell in love with the gloriously rich, raisiny sherry called Pedro Ximénez. I've used it to make this addictive ice cream ever since, although any sweet, syrupy dessert sherry would make a suitable alternative. Italian Marsala makes a fabulous substitute too. For a special touch, soak a few extra raisins to serve with the ice cream.

Put the raisins in a bowl and pour over the sherry. Set aside for as long as possible to plump up and flavour the raisins.

Put the mascarpone, milk and sugar in a bowl and whisk until thick and smooth. Churn in an ice cream machine until the ice cream is almost frozen. Add the soaked raisins and sherry and continue churning until the mixture is completely frozen. Transfer to a freezer-proof container and freeze until ready to serve.

If you are making the ice cream without a machine, follow the instructions on page 8 and fold in the raisins and sherry just before returning the ice cream to the freezer for the final time.

100 g raisins

100 ml sweet sherry, such as Pedro Ximénez

250 g mascarpone cheese

250 ml whole milk

150 g caster sugar

an ice cream machine (optional)

SERVES 4–6

liquorice ice cream

I always justify a second portion of this unusual ice cream by reminding myself that liquorice contains a good dose of vitamin E, plus B vitamins and valuable trace elements. It tastes fantastic too.

150 g liquorice, chopped into small pieces

600 ml double cream

1–2 whole star anise

100 g Demerara sugar

4 egg yolks, beaten

300 ml whole milk

an ice cream machine (optional)

SERVES 6

Put the liquorice pieces in a saucepan, add the cream and star anise and heat gently until the liquorice has almost dissolved. Transfer to a food processor, add the sugar and blend until smooth.

Put the egg yolks and milk in a clean saucepan and stir over low heat until the mixture has thickened. Add it to the mixture in the processor and blend again.

Let the mixture cool completely, then chill if possible. Churn in an ice cream machine until frozen and then transfer to a freezer-proof container and freeze until ready to serve.

If you are making the ice cream without a machine, follow the instructions on page 8.

peppermint humbug ice cream

This is minty, crunchy and a must-try ice cream for all peppermint humbug fans. It's also good made with the sort of candy-striped peppermint rock I used to love as a little girl on trips to the seaside. It's another favourite in my house. But please don't breathe a word to my dentist.

250 g mascarpone cheese

250 ml whole milk

150 g caster sugar

150 g mint humbugs, coarsely crushed

an ice cream machine (optional)

SERVES 6

Put the mascarpone, milk and sugar in a bowl and whisk until thick and smooth. Churn in an ice cream machine until the mixture is almost frozen and then add the crushed humbugs. Continue churning until completely frozen. Transfer to a freezer-proof container and freeze until ready to serve.

If you are making the ice cream without a machine, follow the instructions on page 8 and fold in the crushed humbugs just before returning the ice cream to the freezer for the final time.

pineapple and fresh mint ice cream

Pineapple and custard have always made a great match – especially when the custard is rich, eggy and infused with real vanilla. Alternatively, omit the vanilla and substitute a little fresh mint and the combination is utterly sublime too. Use a good, ripe, fragrant pineapple; the flesh of an under-ripe pineapple will be sinewy when blended and give the ice cream a stringy, grainy texture.

1 large, ripe pineapple

250 g mascarpone cheese

3 tablespoons Malibu liqueur or white rum

200 ml whole milk

4 egg yolks

150 g caster sugar

a small bunch of mint, finely chopped

an ice cream machine (optional)

SERVES 4–6

Peel the pineapple and remove the tough woody core. Chop the flesh and put in a food processor or blender. Add the mascarpone and Malibu and blend until smooth. Set aside.

Heat the milk in a saucepan until it reaches boiling point. Put the eggs and sugar in a bowl and beat until pale and creamy. Pour the hot milk over the eggs, stir until smooth, then return to the stove and cook over low heat, stirring constantly, until the custard has thickened, taking care not to let it overheat and scramble.

Let the custard cool completely, then add to the puréed pineapple mixture. Add the chopped mint and mix well. Churn in an ice cream machine until frozen, then transfer to a freezer-proof container and freeze until ready to serve.

If you are making the ice cream without a machine, follow the instructions on page 8.

malibu and coconut ice cream

This is a creamy dream of an ice cream – it isn't churned in a machine, but has a lovely light texture provided by whipped egg whites – reminiscent of Italian semifreddo. Serve it in scoops, or make in a loaf tin or terrine mould and cut it into slices to serve with wafer-thin slices of fresh pineapple.

Put the egg whites and sugar in a bowl and beat until stiff and glossy. Put the coconut milk powder, mascarpone, Malibu and 100 ml water in a bowl and whisk until smooth. Carefully but thoroughly fold in the egg white mixture. Transfer to a freezer-proof container and freeze overnight.

3 egg whites

150 g caster sugar

90 g coconut milk powder

250 g mascarpone cheese

3 tablespoons Malibu liqueur

SERVES 4–6

southern comfort, saffron and ginger ice cream

Orange blossom honey works particularly well in this gorgeous, saffron-scented ice cream, but if you have difficulty finding it, use any clear, light, flowery honey instead – a strong-tasting honey will drown the delicate balance of flavours.

300 ml whole milk

a good pinch of saffron threads

4 egg yolks

150 g caster sugar

4 tablespoons orange blossom honey

4 tablespoons Southern Comfort

250 ml mascarpone cheese

100 g crystallized ginger, coarsely chopped

an ice cream machine (optional)

SERVES 6

Pour the milk into a saucepan and add the saffron threads. Bring to the boil, turn off the heat and leave to infuse for at least 30 minutes.

Put the egg yolks and sugar in a bowl and whisk until light and creamy. Return the milk to the boil and pour it over the egg mixture, stirring until smooth. Return the custard to the stove and cook over a low heat, stirring constantly, until it has thickened, taking care not to let the mixture overheat. Stir in the honey and Southern Comfort.

Let cool completely, then whisk in the mascarpone until thoroughly blended and smooth. Churn in an ice cream machine until almost frozen, then fold in the crystallized ginger. Continue to churn until the mixture is completely frozen, then transfer to a freezer-proof container and freeze until ready to serve.

If you are making the ice cream without a machine, follow the instructions on page 8 and fold in the ginger just before returning the ice cream to the freezer for the final time.

easy apricot ice cream

This is such an easy recipe to make, that I always feel as if I'm cheating, but in reality the season for good, sweet apricots is so short, that apricot conserve gives a consistently better flavour than fresh fruit – you can have a little taste of summer every month of the year. The quality of the conserve is crucial to the recipe's success: always check the label, and choose a first-rate conserve with at least 55 g of fruit in every 100 g of jam.

250 g mascarpone cheese

200 ml whole milk

100 g caster sugar

250 g apricot conserve

an ice cream machine (optional)

SERVES 4–6

Put the mascarpone, milk, sugar and 200 g of the conserve in a bowl and whisk until thick and smooth. Churn in an ice cream machine until almost frozen, then fold in the remaining apricot conserve to give a ripple effect. Continue churning until completely frozen. Transfer to a freezer-proof container and freeze until ready to serve.

If you are making the ice cream without a machine, follow the instructions on page 8 and fold in the remaining apricot conserve just before returning the ice cream to the freezer for the final time.

blueberry streusel ice cream

Streusel means 'sprinkle' in German. Delicious and crunchy, it is a crumbly topping made of flour, sugar, butter and spices. I use dried blueberries in this ice cream rather than fresh, because they plump up so nicely when soaked in the vodka. They give a lovely chewy texture and contrast beautifully with the crisp streusel.

100 g dried blueberries

3 tablespoons vodka

250 g mascarpone cheese

250 ml whole milk

100 g caster sugar

streusel

100 g unsalted butter

150 g plain flour

100 g light muscovado sugar

2 tablespoons chopped walnuts

a baking sheet

an ice cream machine (optional)

SERVES 4–6

Put the blueberries in a small bowl, sprinkle with vodka and set aside to soak.

To make the streusel, preheat the oven to 180°C (350°F) Gas 4. Put the butter, flour and sugar in a bowl and rub with your fingers until the butter is evenly incorporated and the mixture forms chunky crumbs. Add the walnuts and spread the mixture in an even layer over a baking sheet. Bake for 10–15 minutes until crisp and golden, then remove from the oven and let cool completely.

Put the mascarpone, milk and sugar in a bowl and whisk until thick and creamy. Churn in an ice cream machine until the ice cream is almost totally frozen. Add the blueberries, vodka and the streusel chunks, and continue churning until the mixture is completely frozen. Transfer to a freezer-proof container and freeze until ready to serve.

If you are making the ice cream without a machine, follow the instructions on page 8 and fold in the blueberries, vodka and streusel crumbs just before returning the ice cream to the freezer for the final time.

lemon yoghurt ice cream

A light, zingy yoghurt-based ice cream is lovely to serve with ripe summer berries, but my son Tim loves a huge scoop simply served in a cone. Do choose a good-quality, creamy, full-fat yoghurt or the ice cream will be far too acidic and the texture too icy.

500 ml full-fat plain yoghurt

grated zest and freshly squeezed juice of 2 unwaxed lemons

100 g caster sugar

an ice cream machine (optional)

SERVES 4–6

Put the yoghurt, lemon zest and juice and sugar in a bowl and stir until smooth. Churn in an ice cream machine, then transfer to a freezer-proof container and freeze until ready to serve.

Alternatively, to freeze without a machine, see page 8.

yoghurt ices, sorbets and slushes

mango, mint and lime yoghurt ice cream

This makes a fabulous finish to spicy Asian and Indian meals.

Peel the mango and cut the flesh away from the stone. Put the flesh in a food processor, add the sugar, yogurt, lime juice and mint leaves and blend until smooth. Churn in an ice cream machine until frozen. Transfer to a freezer-proof container and freeze until ready to serve.

Alternatively, to freeze without a machine, see page 8.

1 large, very ripe mango

100 g caster sugar

500 ml full-fat plain yoghurt

freshly squeezed juice 1 large lime

a small handful of mint leaves, finely chopped

a food processor

an ice cream machine (optional)

SERVES 4–6

summer berry yoghurt ice cream

Use good, creamy, plain yoghurt for this recipe and you will be rewarded with a delectable ice cream. A tart, low-fat yoghurt will give a sour, acidic flavour and an unpleasant, icy texture. Frozen fruit works well in this recipe too, just thaw them first. They will ooze juice, so there is no need to warm them through.

500 g mixed summer berries, such as strawberries, blackberries and raspberries

150 g caster sugar

500 g full-fat plain yoghurt

a food processor

an ice cream machine (optional)

SERVES 4

Warm the berries and sugar in a saucepan over low heat for several minutes, until the fruit begins to release its juices. Transfer to a food processor and blend to a purée. Push the purée through a fine-meshed nylon sieve to remove the seeds. Stir in the yoghurt.

Churn in an ice cream machine until frozen. Transfer to a freezer-proof container and freeze until ready to serve.

Alternatively, to freeze without a machine, see page 8.

mojito slush

200 g caster sugar

a generous bunch of
mint leaves, very finely
chopped, plus extra
to serve

100 ml Malibu, Bacardi
or other white rum

freshly squeezed juice
of 4 limes

100 ml sparkling water

*an ice cream machine
(optional)*

SERVES 4

A Mojito is a wonderful cocktail made with white rum, fresh mint and lime. Frozen to a smooth, zingy slush, it makes a gorgeous light ice to serve as pudding, or to enjoy outside on a hot sunny day. I usually substitute Malibu for the customary white rum; the subtle hint of coconut adds a really special touch. Take care though, it's so addictive, you can get sozzled on an ice like this.

Put the sugar and 200 ml water in a saucepan and heat until the sugar has completely dissolved. Let the mixture bubble for 1–2 minutes until slightly syrupy. Remove from the heat, stir in the mint and leave to infuse until cold.

Strain the mixture to remove the mint and stir in the Malibu, lime juice and sparkling water. Churn in an ice cream machine until frozen, then transfer to a freezer-proof container and freeze until ready to serve, sprinkled with mint leaves.

Alternatively, to freeze without a machine, see page 8.

vodka, fizz and lemon slush
(lemon colonello)

This is my version of an amazing cocktail-style slush that I tasted with good friends at a lovely beachside restaurant in southern Spain. After a stunning fish-laden paella, we slurped our way through a couple of these lip-smacking concoctions. We were convinced the recipe came special delivery, direct from heaven. I'm not sure what method of divine intervention helped it to reach Los Sardinales, but we were over the moon about being there to intercept it.

100 ml vodka

400 ml sparkling wine, such as Prosecco or Cava

8 scoops lemon sorbet (see method)

150 ml double cream

lemon sorbet

200 g caster sugar

4 juicy, unwaxed lemons

a food processor

an ice cream machine (optional)

SERVES 4

To make the sorbet, put the sugar in a saucepan with 175 ml water. Heat until the sugar has completely dissolved, then let the mixture bubble for 1–2 minutes until slightly syrupy. Remove from the heat, add the grated zest from 2 of the lemons and the juice from all of them. You should be aiming for about 125 ml lemon juice.

Leave the mixture until completely cold, then churn in an ice cream machine until frozen. Transfer to the freezer until ready to serve. If you are making the ice cream without a machine, follow the instructions on page 8.

To make the slush, put the vodka, wine, lemon sorbet and cream in a food processor and blend well. Churn in an ice cream machine until slushy, then serve immediately.

Alternatively, to freeze without a machine, see page 8.

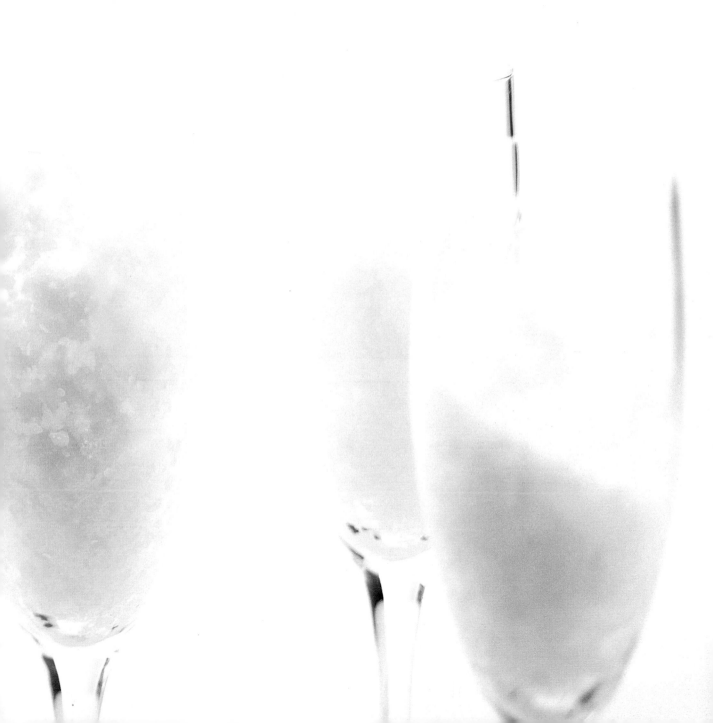

iced lollies

cranberry and orange iced lollies on a stick

Cranberry and orange juices make a fabulous fruity combination, as any devotee of Sea Breeze will attest. Delicious!

600 ml cranberry juice

200 ml freshly squeezed orange juice

200 g caster sugar

iced lolly moulds

MAKES ABOUT 10

Pour the cranberry and orange juices in a bowl, add the sugar and stir until the sugar has completely dissolved. Pour into iced lolly moulds and transfer to the freezer until frozen.

yellow grapefruit iced lollies

600 ml yellow grapefruit juice (about 6 juicy grapefruits)

200 g caster sugar

iced lolly moulds

MAKES ABOUT 10

I've found these delicious, thirst-quenching iced lollies are popular with all ages, and all that vitamin C has to be a bonus. Try this made with pink grapefruit juice too.

Put the grapefruit juice, sugar and 200 ml water in a bowl and stir until the sugar has completely dissolved. Pour into the iced lolly moulds and transfer to the freezer until frozen.

ice cream ice cubes
for sodas

Drop these ice cream ice cubes into tall glasses of lemonade or other soda – to create old-fashioned ice cream sodas. Try topping up real fruit cordials with sparkling water and adding a few cubes; blackcurrant cordial is especially nice. They're also wonderful in sparkling fruit drinks, smoothies and milk shakes.

250 g mascarpone cheese

350 ml whole milk

150 g caster sugar

MAKES 18–24,
depending on size of tray used

Put the mascarpone, milk and sugar in a bowl and whisk until thick and smooth. Transfer the mixture to ice cube trays and freeze until solid.

sauces

fresh berry sauce

This gorgeous raspberry sauce is sublime with vanilla or mascarpone ice cream. The method used to make it can be applied to most fresh summer or autumn berries; strawberries, blackberries and loganberries all work beautifully. Just adjust the sugar to taste.

250 g fresh ripe raspberries
2 tablespoons Framboise liqueur
50 g sugar

a nylon sieve

SERVES 6–8

Put the raspberries in a blender or food processor and purée until smooth. Push the mixture through a fine-meshed nylon sieve to remove the seeds. If your sieve is large and sturdy, you can omit the blender by pushing the berries directly though the sieve with the back of a wooden spoon.

Add the Framboise liqueur and sweeten the purée with the sugar. The exact amount of sugar will vary according to the ripeness of the fruit.

chocolate sauce

This is a rich sauce for lovers of dark chocolate. For a lighter, sweeter alternative, replace the water with double cream.

100 g good-quality dark chocolate, with at least 70 per cent cocoa solids
2 tablespoons golden syrup

SERVES 4

Put the chocolate, golden syrup and 50 ml water in a heatproof bowl set over a pan of gently simmering water (or microwave on HIGH for 1 minute) and stir until smooth. Serve hot or cold.

caramel sauce

This popular sauce will complement many of the ice creams in this book. As with the Caramel Ice Cream (page 14), take care when adding the cream to the hot caramel.

200 g sugar
2 tablespoons golden syrup
300 ml double cream

a sugar thermometer (optional)

SERVES 6–8

Put the sugar and golden syrup in a heavy saucepan over gentle heat and stir until the sugar has completely dissolved. Increase the heat and cook until the mixture turns a dark golden amber colour – 154°C (310°F) on a sugar thermometer. Remove from the heat and carefully stir in the cream, taking care, as the mixture will splutter.

Stir until the caramel has dissolved into the cream. Serve hot or cold.

hot jamaican rum butter sauce

This is every bit as delicious as it is dark. Pour it over the Mascarpone Ice Cream (page 10) and add a little ground spice to complement the ice cream's intended partner. Stir in a pinch or two of finely ground star anise, or a tiny sprinkle of nutmeg or cinnamon. You can change the flavour by using light muscovado instead of dark.

6 tablespoons dark rum
100 g dark muscovado sugar
100 g butter

SERVES 6–8

Put the rum, sugar and butter in a heavy saucepan and stir until the sugar has completely dissolved. Serve hot.

orange and grand marnier sauce

This is glossy and gorgeous.

2 tablespoons liquid glucose
2 teaspoons caster sugar
grated zest and freshly squeezed juice of 2 large, unwaxed oranges
4 tablespoons Grand Marnier
2 tablespoons concentrated orange juice

SERVES 4

Put the liquid glucose and sugar in a saucepan over low heat and stir until the sugar has melted. Add the orange zest, then the Grand Marnier. Carefully light the Grand Marnier with a long match. When the flames die down, add all the orange juice. Bubble lightly over low heat for a few minutes until the sauce reduces and thickens slightly.

butterscotch praline sauce

Crunchy macadamia praline turns an already wonderful toffee sauce into something special. To vary the flavour, try ringing the changes by using different varieties of nuts. I like toasted hazelnuts – but walnuts are wonderful too.

praline

100 g sugar
100 g macadamia nuts

sauce

200 g caster sugar
2 tablespoons golden syrup
300 ml double cream

freshly grated nutmeg, to serve

a pastry brush
a sugar thermometer (optional)
a baking sheet, lightly buttered

SERVES 6–8

To make the praline, put the sugar and 80 ml water in a heavy saucepan over low heat and cook until the sugar has completely dissolved. Use a pastry brush dampened with a little water to wash down the sides of the pan and prevent burning.

Increase the heat and bubble the mixture until it develops a dark amber colour, that is 154°C (310°F) on a sugar thermometer. Stir in the macadamia nuts and immediately spoon the mixture onto the prepared baking sheet. Let cool completely, then break into small pieces.

To make the sauce, put the sugar and golden syrup in a heavy saucepan over a gentle heat and stir until the sugar has completely dissolved. Turn up the heat and cook until the mixture turns a dark golden amber colour – 154°C (310°F) on a sugar thermometer. Remove from the heat and carefully stir in the cream until the caramel has dissolved and the sauce is smooth. Stir in the praline. Serve hot or cold with nutmeg on top.

index